# THE PORTAGE POETRY
# SERIES

Series Titles

*Fulgurite*
Catherine Kyle

*Bowed As If Laden With Snow*
Megan Wildhood

*Always a Body*
Molly Fuller

*Silent Letter*
Gail Hanlon

*New Wilderness*
Jenifer DeBellis

*The Body Is Burden and Delight*
Sharon White

*Bone Country*
Linda Nemec Foster

*Not Just the Fire*
R.B. Simon

*Monarch*
Heather Bourbeau

*The Walk to Cefalù*
Lynne Viti

*The Found Object Imagines a Life: New and Selected Poems*
Mary Catherine Harper

*Naming the Ghost*
Emily Hockaday

*Mourning*
Dokubo Melford Goodhead

*Messengers of the Gods: New and Selected Poems*
Kathryn Gahl

*After the 8-Ball*
Colleen Alles

*Careful Cartography*
Devon Bohm

*Broken On the Wheel*
Barbara Costas-Biggs

*Sparks and Disperses*
Cathleen Cohen

*Holding My Selves Together: New and Selected Poems*
Margaret Rozga

*Lost and Found Departments*
Heather Dubrow

*Marginal Notes*
Alfonso Brezmes

*The Almost-Children*
Cassondra Windwalker

*Meditations of a Beast*
Kristine Ong Muslim

Praise for
*Fulgurite*

"These ethereal poems exist within the mysterious, magical realm of fairytale. Fluid and porous, they have a witchy, spellbound nature. These pieces float."

—Allison Titus
author of *High Lonesome*

"Catherine Kyle's *Fulgurite* is a haunted and haunting collection of poetry that grapples with what it means to survive, as a girl and as a woman, in a world of sexual violence, climate disaster, and late capitalism. This book is also obsessed with magic and offers a rich shapeshifting variety of forms magic can take: a glitter camo backpack; an angel of cohesion as well as of dissociation; ghost girls; Sailor Moon; idiosyncratic and feminist retellings of classic fairy tales; and the speaker's own multilayered and polyphonic soul. Here is a poet who understands metaphor as deep transformation, whose lines strike like lightning and fuse to startle us into truth at once spiritual and politically vital."

—Chen Chen
author of *When I Grow Up I Want to Be a List of Further Possibilities*

"Catherine Kyle is a writer I have long admired, a poet of vast imagination and resonant intricacies. Her work in the domestic and fantastic is essential to our age. Kyle's poems enrich the real and usher in a bright unreal, engage both the instinct and the intellect. We are fortunate to have Kyle's many-faceted constructions in the world."

—Jennifer Militello
author of *The Pact*

"Kyle's latest book is a 'sequined celebration,' delectable with rubies, nightgown silk, bread batter and red-winged blackbirds, angels, hillsides of blueberries and 'hot melted nectar.' Turn it over and the book aches: survivals, ecocide and extinction grief, endless social media and search engine results, 'grinning' flames, 'blushing death.' *Fulgurite* walks beside us, a 'star-specked' companion, into the radiant thicket. Beware, be there, be where the lightning touches."

—Emily Corwin
author of *Sensorium*

"In Catherine Kyle's *Fulgurite*, purgatory is a place where all the mirrors 'show women whose eyes flicker / fire opal in the five a.m. light.' A girl in a glitter camo backpack becomes a symbol for what Kyle calls 'species grief.' Twilight sings through a transparent woman. Aunties come as foxes and owls. Colors like gunpowder get pressed into bombs. Messages from angels keep the speaker afloat as she enters an age of knowing. Through masterfully painted imagery, Kyle offers hope by showing that a woman can find her power in a world where 'men prowl the streets with enormous polished guns.'"

—Reverie Koniecki
author of *to the god of sore feet and bad backs*

"A book of poetry about seeking beauty and meaning in a disintegrating world. . . . Kyle is a spellbinding poet who sometimes makes magic with words: A girl with a glitter camouflage backpack is a 'sequined celebration,' a mouth is a 'cotton candy paint smear,' and God 'lands / as cricket song and hound barks / over dark yards. In moonstone sweat / that curls perfumed hair on her neck.' She vividly describes how the 'turnip of my heart turns a little. rotates wetly,' and the way 'Insects are oublietted in the lampshade.' The result is a tender, endearing narrative of what it means to be human in the modern world. A soulful and often stunning poetry collection."

—*Kirkus Reviews*

# FULGURITE

POEMS

CATHERINE KYLE

Cornerstone Press
*Stevens Point, Wisconsin*

Cornerstone Press, Stevens Point, Wisconsin 54481
Copyright © 2023 Catherine Kyle
www.uwsp.edu/cornerstone

Printed in the United States of America by
Point Print and Design Studio, Stevens Point, Wisconsin

Library of Congress Control Number: 2023931465
ISBN: 979-8-9869663-9-7

Excerpt from *The Lightning Book* by Peter E. Viemeister (MIT Press, 1972).

Cornerstone Press titles are produced in courses and internships offered by the
Department of English at the University of Wisconsin–Stevens Point.

DIRECTOR & PUBLISHER      EXECUTIVE EDITOR
Dr. Ross K. Tangedal          Jeff Snowbarger

SENIOR EDITORS
Lexie Neeley, Monica Swinick, Kala Buttke

PRESS STAFF
Ellie Atkinson, Hannah Fenrick, Patrick Fogarty, Brett Hill, Julia Kaufman, Maria
Scherer, Abbi Wasielewski

*For anyone who has struggled*
*to feel safe and at home in their body.*

Also by Catherine Kyle:

COLLECTIONS
*Shelter in Place*
*Parallel*
*Feral Domesticity*

CHAPBOOKS
*Simple Magic*
*Coronations*
*Saint: A Post-Dystopian Hagiography*
*Gamer: A Role-Playing Poem*
*Flotsam*

# Poems

*If lightning strikes sand of the proper composition, the high temperature of the stroke may fuse the sand and convert it to silica glass. 'Petrified lightning' is a permanent record of the path of lightning in earth, and is called a* fulgurite, *after* fulgur, *the Latin word for lightning.*

—Peter E. Viemeister, *The Lightning Book*

# Glitter Camo Girl

in the metro is a girl with a glitter camo backpack.

imagine—

a camouflage designed to catch the light.     so pretty.

a sequined celebration.

imagine     needing     camouflage like that—

where

would you be hiding? and hiding

from what?

*

the article on megafires     mentions     bodies.          gone,

now.                         acres of bodies.

some animals     might become myths,     things     we tell

our children about.

imagine     needing     protection from something

as common as fire,     continent-wide.

*

a student in the metro     says to his friend:     *last summer,*

*I built a machine gun.*

imagine          other nouns     that noun could be:

*last summer,     I built a pillow fort. a tree house.*

*last summer,    I built better friendships.*

*last summer,    I built a basketful of canned food.*

*I left it on my brother's front porch.*

a girl in the metro in a glitter camo backpack.   disguised.

disguised      as what?

\*

is there a name        for this feeling?

not personal grief—            but species grief,

                              a global grief,

expanding.

the turnip of my heart        turns a little.   rotates wetly.

everywhere, the odor      of ash.

\*

the headline hovers over      a photograph of polar bears

ripping open garbage bags.    the shine of old Coke cans.

I do not click the headline. I do not click the headline.

but I think I catch the words

*extinction grief.*

\*

all things end.

some say, *this isn't    unusual.    unspecial—    unspecial we are, in our grief.*

a girl in a glitter camo backpack is holding

her tall father's hand.  a child. a schoolgirl.

she looks young to be wearing        combat chic, but then,

sometimes I want to disappear, too.

                              unsure how to live in a body.

\*

who was camouflaging      their babies against

the roar of the fire?      disintegrating trees?

what will camouflage me       against the spin of bullets

emitting from a summer gun

like silver?      like light?

\*

scrolling      and scrolling     through three different apps,

I'm looking—     I'm looking—

for answers.

so many experts. discourse, so quick.                surely,

they must be here somewhere.

I click *like* on babies    and warm bread

and glitter      and lipstick     and new cars

and gravy.

I click *like.*    I click *like.*    my red heart flies

through channels      all monitored by men.

imagine        it bouncing      off satellites' skins—

my heart in space,

then landing in pixels.

*

the planet turns red.   a red heart      in space.

a fire. immaculate      fire.

last summer, I picked off      my sequins      like scales—

and what did I find there?   just raw, aching flesh.

just vulnerable, raw, aching flesh.

    imagine—        if I touch it                to a burner,

what then?      a searing.      an ecocide of cells.

*

a girl in the metro has a glitter camo backpack.

so flashy. so militaristic.

    what kind of landscape      could she be in?

            what kind of land      could demand this?

# Seeker

A woman greets the dusk
in the honey locust tree.
California poppy orange
scuttles there as light.

It combs its long fingers
through the woman's hair.
Swings like a kid's grip
from the branches.

She tightens her bathrobe
and reaches her hand out
into violet air. She is searching
for God. And God lands

as cricket song and hound barks
over dark yards. In moonstone sweat
that curls perfumed hair on her neck.
Everything smells of gardenia.

# Confession

We are chopping onions and I tell you, casually,
about the time when I was nine and I sulked in a tree
on an island in Puget Sound for hours. The other
kids and I had been playing *Star Wars* and a boy

said that he was Luke Skywalker. When my friends
and I played in our concrete schoolyard, it was me
who was always Luke. *You're a girl*, the boy said.
*You have to be Princess Leia*. So I turned on my heel

and left. Barefoot, I climbed a tree that overlooked
salt water. Fortressed myself in its leaves.
I listened to waves foam their lives out on logs
and the scream of alley space fights in the distance.

I sat there in green feeling something like a boy and
something like a girl, something like an unknown world.
That was the same summer I fell off a rope swing
onto a wet branch that lodged in my foot. A doctor had

to extract the wood with an implement that looked
like pliers. But I didn't flinch or cry out—in fact,
I watched him pull. Hands gripping crinkling paper of
the elevated bed. *I have never told anyone this*,

I tell you. How I haunted that tree for hours.
Caught between fury and nonchalance. Learning
the quiet of myself. The way silence can be
a sanctuary. But these are power outage times,

though our lightbulbs still hum. By power
outage rules, we offer secrets. Steam rises
between us from the boiling silver pot. A substance
existing in two states at once: liquid and vapor.

Reminding us it's possible. It doesn't just
have to be one. I sweep, with my clean knife,
chopped onion into water. The fragments bubble,
stirred-up moons, now visible, now gone.

## Pomegranate Seeds

The woman deflates in a wicker chair
on the front porch watching the sun set.

Her hair and the straw crosshatch of her
hat glow orange in the tangerine light.

Her garnet fingernails pluck
small seeds from the cove of a split

pomegranate. They glint as they dart through
the din of mosquitoes up and into her mouth.

My own fingers scream against the grated
screen door, behind which I stand in mute

overalls. All of the blood in my twelve-year-old
body cannot save the woman from Hades.

I count with dread as her lips swallow seeds—
ten, fifteen, thirty—wanting to tell her the more

she consumes, the longer she will have to stay.
She does not know the story of Persephone.

She does not know how much I want
to smack the fruit from her hand, to shatter

the seeds against the spotless white house with its
arrogant, terrible grin. I want to see the dark

smear run down its clean side with dripping,
hideous purple, a retort to the lavender dents

Hades leaves on the woman's delicate heart.
I want to claw that smug grin right off its face.

But I think she has had enough of smacks
and claws, this woman, so I open the screen

door, sit down beside her, and brush
the hair from her eyes. I remove the

death fruit from her cold palm
with love and begin to tell her the story.

## Singing Ghost

one ghost asks another why
she always sings in twilight.

opalescent form resounding:
lavender, star-specked.

*oh*, she sighs. *it's not so much
that I sing in the twilight.*

*I just become transparent
and the twilight sings in me.*

# The Angel of Dissociation
# Comes to Collect Me: Age 12

The angel taps at the sliding glass door
and beckons. Behind her, the night sky

is velvet flecked with sharpened
shards of gold. The girl rises

from the computer chair, undoes
the deadbolt, steps into cold air. Silent,

the two of them pick blueberries
that press against the fence. Their hands

run sticky. Their teeth stain blue. Still chewing,
they roll their cuffs, dip their feet into the pool.

The girl hugs her arms across her
Sailor Moon shirt. Stares as her chipped neon toes

kick, submerged. Says, *Online, some guy
just asked if I knew how to—*

*Shh.* The angel puts a finger to her lips.
She braids the girl's hair, berry juice

smearing strands. *Do not let them
strip you of infinity*, she says.

## Seeking Survival: Cinderella

The carriage was magnificent, a sugar egg,
a bauble. So buffed it shone, a moon in nylon
hurtled down the path. A comet parting

trees as sharp as lionesses' jawlines, dripping
glitter from its spokes: a river of crushed quartz.
I might have swallowed porcelain walls like

buttery meringue, my dress a bluebell popped
with satin, rubies on my hips. *I'm sorry,*
said the old enchantress. *It is just illusion.* Mice all

scattered to the corn, cufflinks unfurled as smoke.
Godmother, keep the chalky wigs, the corsets
and cosmetics. Grant me cindered bloomers, trade

this glass for calloused heels. Shudder this pumpkin
to enormous, let me dig my nails in it. Latched,
a driver in a pulpy shell, a grinning heart.

# Small City Garden

I want an auntie who comes in the form of a fox.
An auntie whose fur glows copper and amber

as she swims through mist and light. Gliding
down the blue of the spruce in my yard

as if it is a queenly waterslide. I want an auntie
who comes in the form of an owl, her sharp

talons kneading the woolly thyme like yarn.
An auntie who whispers, *Come outside and see*

*what's growing here.* Who gestures to the raised beds,
their pebbles and tilth. I cannot see it

yet. My breath fogs up the glass.
My fingerprints are cold.

I lost two aunties: one on each side of the family.
Both stillborn.

My mother's older sister with her hair like a fox.
My father's younger sister with the eyes like an owl.

The kitchen timer dings, and like a woman snatched
from the spell of a hypnotist's swinging watch,

I move from the back door. The ghosts
are pawing loudly tonight. The absence soaring darkly.

I need to put on my oven mitts—really,
what rises is too hot to touch.

# Hearth

I have drunk all the milk in the house
again. Your coffee is a pupil sheathed
in green ceramic. Your fingers hook
its handle and its wet surface fractures
white light from the gold ceiling bulbs.
Insects are oublietted in the lampshade.
Its funnel a triangular furrow of dry shell.
I am wearing my apron, the red one
I wore when my high heel slid up
your thigh in March, in rain. I am pulling
cinnamon buns out of the oven. My mitts
warm. My cheeks flushed and red, my heart
red. I slather glaze on one and bite it,
still scorching. I say, *Have a nice day, dear.*

# Purgatory

All the mirrors in this house show women whose eyes flicker
fire opal in the five a.m. light. The faucet is running. The water
runs cold. The veins in our wrists hit the water. Pulse cold.

All the bedsheets in this house are summer sky blue. Embalm us
in wildflower petal hues. Colors like gunpowder I could press
into bombs. Could sculpt them with my hands, press them round

as gingersnaps. Could swallow them, erupt into suns.
Stick out your tongue: let me see what you have eaten. I see: red
and pink pigments, too. You cup my face. My fire opal ring catches

in your hair. We tug. It will not come loose. So we stay like this:
your hands move to the silk of my nightgown. Me staring
at the cotton candy paint smear of your mouth.

## Domesticity

I am pacing in the bedroom and with every footstep,
lupins bloom through floorboards, mauve and blushing blue.
Lily of the valley winds its way down from the ceiling fan.
Dandelions blossom from the pane of my hand mirror.
Soon, I wade calf-deep in them. I tousle my hair. I keep
pacing. Petals fall from rafters like the ash from some great

barn. The horses, I am sure, have all escaped, muscles taut.
Hyacinth is fluttering from all the dresser drawers. I lie
on a bed made of poppies. Lord, if you cover me,
a shadow shaped like a man, and trace with your thumbnail
the line that knits my ribs, expect me to unzip. Expect
to find not blood, but hot melted nectar there.

# Home/world

green curtains, I think,        would liven up the room.

I Google, *green leafy   curtains.*

      and pastels and vibrant tones,    exuberant,    verdant,

eruptions of color form in squares on my screen. infinity. infinity

of choices.

I am building a nest. I want my home       to resemble a forest.

something un-human.

I wonder, though, if there can be any

real escape     from us.

\*

*green leaves wind around the windowpanes—    they rustle there,*

*blocking out my neighbor's        motion-sensing light.*

\*

after Twitter makes excuses for     the national gun fetish,

or the famous pussy-grabber quote circles again,

I look up fluffy bedspreads. I look up fluffy comforters. I want

to be comforted.     the economy doesn't comfort me.

my ability to buy things

doesn't do it.

there's this inability          to distract myself.

no matter what the thread count,

it leaks in, see.

it leaks in,      a cold draft,    chilling.

*

the headline says the oceans        are warming at the rate

of five atomic bombs

being dropped in every second.

it took me      a second

to Google this:      *oceans warming,      five atomic bombs.*

I had hoped that it might be          per year.

the company ships me my new bathrobe      in two easy days.

172,800 seconds.

*it's too hot,* I say      when the pink fabric comes.

*it's actually too—*      *it's too hot.*

*

*vines part and eyes glimmer out from shadowed gardens.*

*the twinkle lights we've strung there*

*flicker and go out.*

*

it will not save me. it will not save me.

                    this cutely-patterned bedsheet. I ask

too much of it.      ask it to be a shield.

meanwhile, a gunman opens fire

in my hometown.           I text five friends and all say,

*which shooting do you mean?*      *you know,*

*there were two today.*

\*

I cannot do anything     for creatures in the ocean.

the ones right now,

the price that's paid    for global procrastination.

the almighty twiddling of thumbs.

\*

          *out the window, something hairy,*

          *someone growling with long fangs—*

          *a beast from the last mass extinction*

          *scratches at my door.*

          *I slide the glass pane open*

          *and offer him an apple.*

          it's local,    *I say.*

                            I'm so sorry.

\*

I cannot go and rescue the mother orangutan

who swats at bulldozers       while clinging to a tree.

a leafless tree, against a cloudless sky.

the system needs to catch up.       needs to catch on.

I donate to a charity       and close the browser tab.

                    what else can I       do?

\*

my cat has this register       she goes to when she's hungry.

a higher voice, a chirping trill       she uses to work me.

they say domesticated cats       learned to mimic toddlers

to access human instincts

to feed.

this small voice cries   in the universe

                    and stares me

                              right in the eye.

                              right in the eye.

how wonderful it is, then,

                    to feed her.

## Supplication to She-Ra

Goddess of the glowing blade
who sees the best in everyone,

help me make the kind of world
that I can stand to live in.

I purchase a ring forged in the shape
of your helmet on Etsy, with five

-star reviews. I wear it to make
myself braver, kinder. I wear it to make

a grappling hook
I can sink in the face of this cliff.

## The Angel of Dissociation
## Comes to Collect Me: Age 18

The angel pulls up on a hillside at dusk.
Purple hits the mountains like a dumped

can of light, a spray of translucent
gleam. The girl she seeks

is painted, like them, half orange, half violet
as the sun pares night. Their shadows

meld as the angel's wheels scratch concrete.
The girl's sandaled marching halts.

*What is it?* the angel asks, looking at her red
cheeks, the arms folded over her chest.

*Two men*, the girl starts, extending one
finger. Her gaze follows its point.

—*catcalled me.* Her tank top is punctuated
with white. Baby's breath patterns and leaves.

The sunset dips the fields in gold. She is
not wearing a bra. *Your first time?* the angel asks.

The girl quickly nods. The vineyards are bursting
with grapes and birdsong. Marigolds bustle

with bees. *Get in,* the angel beckons.
*And welcome to the liminal. This feeling is a*

*harbor*
*of holy, lost girls.*

# Fairy Tale with an AR-15

I should not have been surprised that the spider in my hair
turned out to be a breadcrumb. Nor by the apples
that tumbled from the tree, each looking like one bite

had been taken from it, tooth-marred and exact. As if
the witch had forgotten which fruit held the poison
and decided to try all of them herself. The apples

like Renaissance cherub cheeks: rosy and round and
delicious. Men prowl the streets with enormous, polished
guns. They cradle them like I might a baguette. And I should

not be surprised when the dragon scorches the wheat fields
to dust. The orchards to ash. I should not be surprised by
my wandering, barefoot, trying to pick seeds from all that wreckage.

The compass in my pocket is silent for once. It does not know
what to say either. We watch as the sword in the stone is
repainted with a mural of a stake in the heart of the world—

one with a silencer, one with a trigger. It happened
so silently until we heard it: the crackling our banners,
our very own rooftops. If there were a spider living

in my hair, I would place him on the rose bush
growing by the sea. I would say to him, *Spin thread to suture
this chasm. Lord knows I cannot see the other side from here.*

How to Tell the Angel of Cohesion That the Boy She
Keeps Asking About Did Something Bad to You

Pick the day the two of you walked side by side in the park,
your silk blouse white, your skirt blood red. The day the
trees cast pollen down like scads of shooting stars. When
the angel asks, *How is that boy—the one with the fancy car? I
can't remember his name,* say, *The truth is, he was a pterodactyl
that gobbled up my lungs.*

Or pick the day when she said, *That boy who moved out
east—drove a Lexus or something—whatever happened to
him?* Smile and say, *His lungs filled with pollen. He drowned
in tree spores. I think he's a park with a lake now.*

Or pick the day when she said, *That boy you used to play
with—who did he dress as?* Remember the two of you
dressed as mortal enemies. His character tried to kill yours.
But didn't succeed.

Or pick the day you played, the braid down your back a
bright pendulum, a swinging snake. Consider how you
posed in combat stances for photos. Then actually spar. He
will jab with his fist, so conjure a blade. Lightning will
surge through every cell until you are impossible to touch.
A human electric fence. Show the angel this. Point to the
crackling blue. Say, *This is how I live now.*

Or pick the day when you drew on the boy's arm. A tem-
porary tattoo. Freeze the frame and tell the angel, *It hasn't
happened here yet. But still, I should use something stronger.*
When your marker hits his skin, let pollen pour out in-
stead of dark ink. Let it crawl up his elbow and swallow
his shoulder whole. Let bees come to collect it, alight on
his hand and his wrist—a bracelet buzzing with tongues, a
swarming, million-legged glove.

Say to the angel, *That boy became honey, I think. He was transfigured. Yes, if I remember, he moved to the field just outside of town. His car became honeycomb. He became goo. His memory: just sweet goo now.*

# Seeking Survival: Little Red Riding Hood

Firs as green as guts
of emeralds dipped in oceans
scratch my cheeks. Bark
and pitch beneath my shoes
a crunching susurrus.

And paths are meant
to be strayed from—isn't
that how we get new paths?
Wasn't this planet pathless
once? Wasn't it *choose your own?*

There is something
breathing here, an old thing,
ancient. Fur as gray
as silver caught in moonlight
strokes my hair.

Forest panting
on my throat. I shed my gloves,
my stockings. Wander in
the clearing, touching
sap and pinecone teeth.

I let my basket trail
off, confections littering
woods, pink glint. Press
my palms into the tilth.
Feel my eyes go gold.

## The Angel of Dissociation
## Comes to Collect Me: Age 13

The angel and the girl lie under a worn quilt,
eating goldfish crackers. The girl points out

the heroes on the posters on her walls.
Heroes contained in bodies contained in body

-revealing clothes. *I'm still not sure
how to live in a body*, the girl says,

pink skirts reflecting
in her eyes. *But I think*

*it's the being not-seen that does it—that
annihilates.*

# Baby Ghost

*I torched it*, the ghost says, kicking
her feet from a finely carved
ghost highchair. the other ghosts

stop and thumb their chins
and furrow their ghost brows.
they can't imagine

why such a nice child would
do something so destructive.
they can't imagine

where she would get kindling
in the first place. they point at
each other. *was it you?*

*you who let her
have that match?* the baby laughs,
claps loud ghost palms.

all her hair
is made of fire.
all her body, too.

# Seeking Survival: Vasilisa the Beautiful

By the light of the skull
whose sockets flicker
amber, scarlet scalding,

the house that fanged
me through with fear
becomes a pile of char.

*Such gentle blessings*
*will not serve you,*
the old woman scolded,

brushing corn
from the cloth doll
my mother

gave me. Muttering,
she handed me
grinning flame.

I did not know
its will. I thought
it would light

my way, did not know
it would stare infernos.
I step from the smoldering

beams, the lumber
of this hut
erupted.

Into freedom. Hair incensed
with ash. A question
mark. A study

in contrasting blessings.
Girlish, fearsome.
Blushing death.

## What I Mean

What I mean when I say *I need to get out* is I need to feel the tremors of music earthquaking my lungs. That my heart-boat has filled with some kind of fluid and I am bailing it out. That this feeling can only be cured, some nights, by high-heeled black boots and glitter. That when I put on my eyeshadow with glitter, you had better watch out. That this means I am a kind of monster polishing its fangs. That I will scour the village for flowers, eat them straight off the oak table doilies, if it will mean digesting beauty. Mean salving this aching sweet tooth. It means you cannot trust me, these nights, to not run my claws down the bricks of an alley like keying one enormous car. It means if I do not, I will be an Etch-A-Sketch, swirling, Odysseus' satchel of winds. That something will howl, press out of my fingertips, latch to all I touch like ink.

\*

What I mean when I say *Forget it* is that I am walking through hallways of mirrors, none of which have reflections. I mean I am walking, mouth tightly covered with lengths of purple cloth. That my hands are in mittens, three pairs of mittens. Fumbling toward the glass. That I am a firefly trapped in a jar with no punctured lid holes. A thing that buzzes, glows, and wanders, circular, on its round track. You say, *I don't know what that means. When you say that, I don't understand.* What I mean is that I am the heroine of a B-movie, the one in ripped taffeta, hurtling into the lava. Shaking the bars of a rust cage. What I mean is that maybe you are the sword, or maybe, actually, I am the sword, or the hairpin that jimmies the padlock. What I mean is the lava is scalding my skirt and I had better decide.

\*

What I mean when I say *Nothing* is my words have fallen like silver circles into the couch's furrow. Have tumbled down the grinning storm drain like the nose stud I once lost. It glimmered—*twinkle, little stud*—and ricocheted to water. Once these things are lost, they're lost. Leaves that spill to gutters melt to sludge, become soft matter. Pens that slip behind the hulks of fridges eat their own ink. What I mean is things are not the same once they've slithered down the sink. Though what survives the trip to the sewer doesn't have to languish. We've all heard stories of the gators basking in the slime. Or creatures crawling out of manholes in the nightshade-blue gloam. Rifling through the battered trashcans. Dancing in the streets.

# The Angel of Dissociation
# Comes to Collect Me: Age 23

The angel pulls up in front of the nightclub. Wet streets
shine with oil and stoplight scarlet,

viridian, gold. She rolls down her window.
Her lipstick is immaculate. She turns

the radio down. *Come,* she says
to the girl who folds

her coat around her waist
like a pair of drenched wings.

Wide-eyed, the girl clicks open
the passenger door,

slumps into the car. The angel's
engine is thrumming with heat. Raindrops

smack the thin roof. Low-volume
saxophone wrestles with static.

The angel keeps her
fresh manicure on the wheel,

eyes the rider beside her:
fishnets. Glitter

embedded in red lips. Smell
of hairspray. Sweat.

*You find what you were looking for?*
the angel asks, softly. *I'd say*

*it was a hit,* the girl replies.
*They all thought I had fun.*

*That number is*
*a knife across a palm, but*

*the feathers and the sequins—*
*they make it look like fun.*

# Seeking Survival: The Little Mermaid

It starts with a song. You are beachcombing at night, sand opalescent, waves the color of ink. And there she is, perched on a flat rock crusted with bird shit and barnacles, humming something by The Cure, fin abrupt as a loose tooth. Hair more violet than sunrise. She turns when she hears the *shh* of your footfall. Not startled, as you'd expected. She twirls a Marlboro through fingers that shine just faintly with slime, nails painted sparkle-dark but badly chipped from brine. *Got a light?* she asks, and you sit down beside her, denim butt wetted with incessant sea spray. You *flick, flick, flick* the lighter; she leans in close and your heart skips. The paper catches, orange eclipse. Smoke curves upward toward Orion. Pipers skitter by. After this, you start bringing her things—mixed cassette tapes, scented markers, a pleather jacket for her birthday. She exchanges gifts with you—conches, urchins, friendship anklets woven from red kelp. Once, you kiss her cheek as she ties a sand dollar pendant around your neck. She smiles and averts her gaze, laugh all salt and ash. *There is much I want to show you*, you later urge, clutching her damp hands. *Cars, and concerts, and*—you stammer, glancing at her fin. A line appears between her eyebrows. *There is much I want to show you, too—reefs and sunken graveyards. But*—she says, and pats your knee, thrift-store turquoise jangling. *There's a witch*, she starts, and looks you squarely in the pupils. *I hear she could transform you.* Your throat seizes. You shake your head. She laughs, blots out the singeing filter, lowers to the surf. *That's what I thought*, she says. Waves kiss her shoulders. *Yeah, that's what I thought.*

# Family Ghost

ghost girl touches the family
photograph, edges creased, gnawed

by time. runs her pointer
finger down the silky paper

seam. it crosses the breast
of a woman, fold a sash imitating a

quiver. echo of what weaponry
she might have gripped and shot.

ghost girl knows many weapons
are invisible. knows many injuries

are guarded under tongues.
the woman's face is stalwart,

mouth a heart monitor
with no pulse. ghost girl wants

to climb inside, to interview
her teeth.

> *what was your*
> *life like?*

> *what would you have wished*
> *you could demolish?*

> *what would you have saved,*
> *had you power?*

> *how was it,*
> *your pre-ghost?*

## Seeking Survival: The Little Match Girl

a girl throws    a red scarf

around a man's neck

    something like a star in a movie would do

      feeling cute and brave

she pulls the man closer   and says,   *when are you going*

    *to figure it out?*

the fringe drips down his shoulders

    his grin is guillotined

    as such, it cannot     reply

*

*first match: apparition*

the Angel of Denial   has a plague doctor mask

it's sequined

she's auraed in        my favorite perfume

I clutch at her plaid coat       my face hits her boot

already, she's dissolving       wet sugar under nails

I pull down my collar

and show her the cut

where the wolf,      he got me—

his long, incising fangs

I place her gloved fingers      here   in the wound

where my rib slid out

just like a tooth pulled

just gone      like a xylophone key

I squint      she is just mist now

she kneels down      a rose blooms

*and what*      *were you wearing?*   she says

*

*second match: apparition*

eating mall pizza      with the Angel of Deflection

who sat there   texting a friend   with my phone

I tried it      again:

*my chest*—   *something is gone*—

she joked behind her plague mask   snapping her bubblegum

teasing her hair      with my brush

and after that I swallowed it

down like some huge fish

                        it settled in the well          of my
belly
           oxidizing

           where now it is rust

                        and a searing turquoise blue

*

some say the poultice     in the scythe beaks of the masks

actually helped          to keep the plague away

the bouquet of spices       that kept the scent of death out

spared them from having          to deal

*

managing guilt over soggy potatoes

most solid thing I'd eaten in weeks

                        *when are you going     to figure it out?*

it ended up taking     another eight years

                        no wonder, then, that she shrank

*

    would you believe this guy     wouldn't even sit next to me

                        on the public bus

he turned his eyes away

the psychic said, *not everyone*

        *can take that bright crown chakra love*

        *that violet shining beacon*

        *to them, incinerates*

and what a spectacular    backfire

*

the same day I finally call the crisis hotline

I go to the optometrist

    the verdict is the same:    your vision    is fine

        *you see it in the distance*

    your vision    about this    is fine

*

*third match: apparition*

I strike what is left in me:    a long,    sunlit rib

    it serves me like a scalding torch    burning out the path

I stride down the road into silhouette woods

as sequined masks with silver ribbons

        flutter to the ground

hear me out, this is no    extinction

# Prom Witch

I just wanted to, like, spike
the red punch with rhododendron.

Not to hurt anybody, just to watch the pink flowers, like,
saturate the juice. I wanted to see their pollen

dissolve and float like tiny gold kelp.
Wanted to smell the tropical fruit punch

mix with garden blooms. The woodchips
and the wetness of a thousand rainy schoolyards,

plus the ardor and the sweat of thirty dance floor
gyms. Sound of bodies pulsing in the dark,

nervously. If I throw a hair tie in and
swirl it with a pom-pom, grass stains, and

anxiety, you'll have my recipe. What
some girls are made of: sugar pink and terror red.

# The Angel of Dissociation
# Comes to Collect Me: Age 19

The angel rides the elevator five floors up
to the dorm room that overlooks the city.

The girl sits on the balcony, wrapped in a blanket.
Papers filled with watercolor smears and tallied calories

flutter on the floor. Wind ruffles their seams.
Orange rinds spiral their shapes at the sky. Night fills up

the gaps in their coats. *Whatever you are looking for*, the angel
says softly, *it cannot be found by unfurling.*

The girl drops the blanket
and takes the angel's hand. *I'm exhausted,*

she says,
*of this self.*

## My Soul Shudders In and Out of My Body
## Like a Microscope In and Out of Focus

I want to watch certain cartoons with you.
Not the bad stuff where breasts get groped
for laughs, but the nourishing stuff, the ones
where girls turn into cats and crystals light
the way. I don't know how to change
the world. I do know how to make good
blueberry pancakes. The secret is in the vanilla.
I know how to weed around the rosemary bush
so that birds swoop down and gobble up the unearthed
bugs. I admit I don't know how to keep this soul
inside of this body. It keeps shifting
out. We joke I am made of three eels and a fog spirit
wrapped in a pink bathrobe. The eels squiggle restlessly,
sniffing out salt water. The fog spirit tugs me toward the foothills
in the north. All those rose hips and prospects
of vanishing. It's an ongoing process to not evaporate.
Can't tell you how difficult it is. *Stay here*, you whisper
into my hair. Holding these fingers
that are somehow mine. My soul flickers in
and out of my body to the beat of the song
in the show we are watching on the laptop raised
on your knees. Rain splatters down from the storm drain, and
although embodiment often feels like a cinched-up ballgown
of thorns, this is pleasant. I sip lemon tea.
I feel your warmth. *I'll try*, I say. *I'll think about it.*

## The Angel of Brunch

The angel pulls her hair up into a bun.
She is wearing flip-flops in my kitchen.
Light filters through the chrysanthemum

curtains and she sizzles two eggs
sunny-side up. She got them from a
friend's backyard chicken. I am standing

beside her mixing citrus bread batter
in a transparent bowl with a wood spoon.
I ask her what is sacred. Everything?

Nothing? The feeling I get when I lock
eyes with someone, and our hearts say
what's in them without speaking? The angel

scratches the back of her neck, pulls the
half-gallon of orange juice from the fridge.
She shakes it, then hands me the measuring

cup, which I hold over the batter as she pours.
*Yes*, she says. *That. But also, you know that
feeling you get when you have to mouth the words*

*to the song on your headphones, even when you're
on a public bus? And the way your cat always
starts on your belly, but slides to the left*

*in the night? Those too*, she says, tapping
the side of the measuring cup
with her plastic spatula's lip. At its touch,

the liquid there burnishes to sunlight,
amber nectar glowing like a floodlamp.
I tilt it and empty out the luminous pulp:

a waterfall of gold, as if we're forging.
I stir and stir the blessing in until
the whole room is radiant.

## Subaquatic

The harbor ghost cooks me seafood linguine. The counter
is littered with garlic and shells. He murmurs that
the white wine sauce is what turns salt
to tang. He is wearing an apron to indulge me,
wipes wet brine on its pinstriped folds. His hands
are coral reefs, chopping each onion. And
candlelight in his long hair. I wind my fingers
into his beard like clownfish seeking refuge.
I kiss him and taste the drowning of dawns.
Moonlit melancholy, cloistering pearls. This man:
a mouth of shipwrecks, an underwater trench.

# Shotgunning

Give me your jaw,
your smoke and your ash—

your chin and the notch
of my thumb are a fit.

Breathe your incense
into my lungs—

I will inhale
while our blurred eyes

lock. I am still tracing
the bone that sleeps

below your left ear,
spattered in hair,

when you pull back,
still open,

a cannon mouth fired,
lips chiaroscuro,

silent
as stars.

# Twilight

The cat comes to the back screen door
and scratches the aluminum. She wants
to be let in. I have no child, so she is
my child, and I dote on her: I kneel to

oblige. There is a gold leaf right below
her left ear in the space where her
eyebrow would be. I brush it with the
backs of my fingers, wanting to clean

my child up. Only it was not a leaf; it was
a spider, and now I have crushed it
carelessly. I brushed it so gently. My cat's
huge pupils take me in as I mouth,

*I'm so sorry.* I did not mean to harm it,
but my fingers were large and clumsy
on its small spider body. What disasters
are stirring in me that I cannot be aware of?

What oblivious damage? And what latent
lightning sits in you? That could tumble
like loose logs off the back of a truck?
If God is a spider, I want to say, *Mercy.* As his,

her, their enormous legs brush across the world.
I want to say, *Spare me,* for I am so small.
I want to say, *Grant me exemption from the cycle
of life and death. I want no part in it.* But God

seems to say, as I water the mint plants,
the discs of sun and moon in the twilight
ocular, *Look at what you sow and
look at what you reap and try to do more*

*of the former.* Mud pools around my feet
in the garden and I hope it will help some
roots below me grow. I am not enough,
but I am trying.

# Eden

You tend to the garden. Your skin glistens
sweat, glazing you a slickened sea creature
come to land. Salt pools on your upper lip.

You lean on your shovel. Your wrists drape
its grip. You brush hair from your eyes, leave
a dirt smudge with your glove, the space

above your eyebrow a canvas met with dust.
The lemon thyme and rosemary are already
in full bloom. Fragrance reaches me inside: I rev,

a motor growls. It seems now I have eaten
all the berries meant for canning. The peaches
too. My lips and hands are mottled with their

juice. The glass jars are still
sanitizing in the steaming pot. I wipe
my kitchen knife on gingham, sopping

my new skirt. I rummage for the scissors
in the overcrowded junk drawer. I have this
sudden craving. Crush of lemon. Sour sun.

# Mosaicists

Everywhere you go, you leave beach glass,
smooth and turquoise. Clouded. Opaque as milk.
Everywhere you go, you leave new shards,

too. Ruby snares. Smoldering flint sparks.
I pluck them from the carpet as though
I am picking berries. As though I am gobbling

breadcrumbs. I gather them in clear jars. They glitter
on the windowpanes. I beachcomb. I navigate by stars.
Singing in my silk slip, I grind them up so finely

in mixing bowls with silver whisks, they rustle there
like sand. I sprinkle them in flowerbeds. They fertilize
the soil there. They shimmer to plead you come home.

## Seeking Survival: The Wild Swans

I refuse to wear the nettle shirt.
The one I once thought I had
to wear, to make you good,
to make you love me.
The one that scratched
my breasts with its thorns until
they were welted and red.
Instead, I take your cable knit
sweater and weave my lilies
through it. Its woolen bends
like braided hair. Its crisscross
river wending. I coil their vines
around your cloth until it looks
like you are blooming. Until
you look like a sculpture retaken
by land in a haunted courtyard.
A bee nestles into your navel.
Two petals mirror your rib cage.
I open you, ripe and twisting
toward sun. I open you.
Feathers take flight.

## Torch

Outside my window is a gold, gold tree.

       Its leaves are not ombré. They are solid

gold. Like a kid might color in       a sun with yellow crayon.

The tree glows like    a holy pyre,

a fluttering liturgical candle.

Set against the opal sky,           wavering. Burning.

A flame I could warm      my hands on.

*

Last autumn, my family packed up   their pets

and fled from the fire    that licked down the trees.

My mother did not    have time to grab her cell phone.

They packed up their pets

and left.    This was after    my brother

went downstairs to get a drink   and the hillside of blackberries

was knocking at the window

in flames.           Almost close enough to touch.

They drove through the night. One cat. Two dogs. Four people.

Driving for their lives.

*

The tree out my window is not a ginkgo tree,

but I like to pretend that it is.

Ginkgo trees, too, produce such light.

Their mermaid-tail leaves brighter than honey.

Before he died, my grandfather        loved ginkgo trees.

He said they dated back

to the dinosaurs and he    admired that resolve.    Survival

for so, so long.

I wish I could interview the *Ginkgo biloba*,    ask it

what it has seen.

Meteors and Ice Age.        Empires and ruin.

A tidal        waltz        of life.

If I could, I would ask it, *What do we do?*

*You've seen it all. What do we do?*

*

The news says some firefighters rescued    a mountain lion cub

who was wandering    alone amid the char.        He was

orphaned,      see.

They named him Captain Cal.        Nurses treated his burns.

In videos online, you can look

into the Captain's eyes.

Imagine what he has seen.

*

My family takes        a video of what the fire did

to their next-door neighbor's siding.

A scorch mark slashes its way across the house.

A hot knife dragging  its ire.

*It tastes like smoke,* they tell me        once they are back home.

*Inside the house. The air,*

*it tastes like smoke.*

*

I have never wanted to believe more      in charms,

in prayers,      in blessings.

My mother's friend says        the small row of stones

that is blessed

helped protect them from the fire.    I do not know how

or why the stones are blessed. Or who blessed them.

But I want it to be true.

*

My grandfather had      this tree in his back yard.

A ginkgo.　　By a hillside

full of nightshade.　　Whenever we'd play blackjack,

he'd gesture to its gold leaves, say,

*Think of that, Cat.*　　*Think of all it has survived.*

*It must know something rare. Something special.*

I'd nod and crunch a pretzel. Study my hand.

The cards adding up to 17.　　At 21 or higher, you lose.

*Hit me*, I'd say.

Pushing my luck. Hoping to beat the odds.

# Beacon

My slate turtleneck has shrunk in the wash.
Now, when I walk, the hem brushes the navel
piercing I once fetched as a lure. In the cramped
dark shop that overlooked the sea. Turning out
girls with jewels in their guts. Sparkling like
anglerfish.

The birch trees lean over a chain link fence
claiming to delineate footpath from shore.
But see here, it ends. Inviting the truth. Inviting
trespass in this river. Take my hand—it is
muddy, this part of the slope. I don't want you
falling in.

In the recurring dream I had as a child that taught
me the meaning of hunger, a man shows up
on the doorstep of a woman who had thought
he was dead. Her heart is stampeding, but she acts
casual. She chatters and heats up the kettle for tea
until she is harpooned with a kiss.

I lied. It wasn't a dream, but a wish, something seen
penciled in storm clouds. The birch trees are peeling
their bark from themselves. And I am an orange
with the rind pulled back—a pulpy orb of a heart.
The gemstone that punctures me glitters through
fabric. A lighthouse. A siren. A song.

## The Angel of Dissociation
## Comes to Collect Me: Age 20

The angel honks twice like an impatient parent
picking the girl up from school. The girl's eyes

refocus, having stared for too long at the rain
on the windshield: a mesh, a clear net. Looking

through the droplets, she sees the angel's car
gleaming like a raven across the parking lot.

The boyfriend has gone inside to buy some things.
The canyon around them is jagged. No green.

The girl opens the car door. Her arm: instantly soaked.
She climbs out and watches the downpour shade

her clothes. Baby blue morphs to lilac dark. Aqua
succumbs to deep sea green. Crusted pawprints

reanimate on fabric, loosening from hardness
to runny, slick mud. Earlier, he'd scolded her:

*Now there is filth where there was beauty*, he had
said, pointing at wet paw smears on silk.

*Bad, bad girl*, he had said, but she couldn't tell
which of them he was chiding: her or the dog.

Stepping over painted lines and dividers, the girl feels
saturated cloth cling to her thighs. Her eye makeup

is rivulets. Her bare feet cake with grit. She touches
her hands to the mud on her skirt. A kind of

high five, a kind of communion: paw-palm,
feral-heart. The angel starts the engine up.

# River Ghost

I want to talk
to the river but
the river is either
silent or roaring. no in
-between, no inside
voice. it pouts
or throws my things.

already it has broken
thirteen teacups wrapped in paper,
gold-kissed rims and
painted cobalt landscapes
jigsaw crunch.

the river does not speak
in words. it speaks
in overflowings. creeping
over sandy shores
and soaking my new boots.

it will not *talk*
  to me, it will not *talk*
to me, it will not *tell*
  me what
it wants. it wants
to be angry, I think. it wants
to Cubist all my mirrors.

*look at me*, it seems to growl.
my face: a rippled blot.

# Seeking Survival: Snow White

You say you want my heart in a box.
A velvet-lined casket, a gold latch.

I spit loam from my tongue, pick the pine
from my cheek where I fell, or more,

descended. Knees to palms to obsequious
damsel: *Do it, if you must.* Shivering spine

and shoulders a knob-throated serpent
with shuddering plumage. Pulsating symmetry

too cute to undo—your huntsman, he faltered,
he fled. His dagger hit the dirt like a star. I puncture

my own breastbone. None may hold my heart
but me. I unlatch, latch the box. Prowl the green,

avoid the cottage, piercing carnivores' gaze. Night
and wind my entourage: a kingdom of the brave.

# The Angel of Dissociation
# Comes to Collect Me: Age 21

The angel's car idles in a fifteen-minute parking spot
outside the coffee shop with vegan maple scones.

The girl comes out, holding a sack of them
and clutching her laptop like a second metal heart.

She is grateful for the angel. *I missed my bus*,
she says. The angel nods. Inside, the leather seats

are warmed by gushing heat vents. Frost has not yet
bitten the windows, but a chill rides the air like

a henchman on a horse. The girl is wearing
yesterday's clothes. *I missed my bus*, she keeps saying.

*And his plane took off. And I don't know who I am.*
Perfume and hotel soap necklace her throat.

The angel sighs and rustles the paper
sack, pulls out a pastry

and gazes at its crust. Scratches its
top sugar with one long

red claw. *You're not as helpless
as you sometimes*

*like to pretend*, the angel says, side
-eyeing her, licking glaze from her nail.

*But you do
like to pretend.*

## Seeking Survival: The Snow Queen

Glass froze like a pick in your eye and lodged there, bleeding disdain. Everything you saw was tinged in red, kaleidoscopic fly eye dipped in contempt. For me, for our home, for this glitter city punched with a boxing glove of light. When I woke and saw the absent aura of your car, slate rectangle dry in the all-else wet concrete, I knew you'd gone missing. Feared you were dead. I must have sent three hundred texts.

When even the broken heart emoji did not bring you back, I zombied to the beach. To the waves that we listened to late at night, as you hushed shushing whispering into my hair. I asked the lapis ocean if you were dead and placed my new heels, red stilettos caked with sand, into the slop of the foam and the salt. They bobbed there. Water slipped into the toes. But the tide did not devour them. It sloshed them back, a hermit crab climbing the leathery arch. This was how I knew you were alive.

I wandered misty dawn streets barefoot then. Purchased fifty roses from the only stall open so early in the day. I left them in all your favorite spots—the coffee shop, the library—in hopes you would see them, would remember the time you washed me in petals and suds. Calling me divine, saying how you feared to touch me. How you thought I would singe your palms. It makes so much more sense now—but how was I to know your body was a field awaiting ice seeds? To burrow, to wriggle there, to sprout?

When I finally find you, the moon has come up. It glints through the window on the ice in your cup. A ripple-face in your liquor. Rose petals fall from my hands and my coat as I trudge through the snow-licked door. Hazy orange sucks the piano keys from a candle on top of the bar. My heels and toes are lilac blue. My hair is white, waist-long now. *I have been searching*, I say, *a long time for you*. You turn and that hideous flash in your eye tells me you are still forged of glass.

Once, I would have been reindeer for you. Would have gladly been bandit or princess. Once, I would have surrendered for you, would have offered my flesh to the crows. Now, I move forward. Your hair is white. Your gums, immaculate scowl. I reach out as if to caress your cheek, then pilfer the shard from your glare. A tiny shard—a thing so small, it spider-crack-shattered our lives. I place it onto my tongue like a wafer and crunch it between my molars. I spit the fine grains into your drink. I put my stilettos on, braid my hair. Take my roses back.

# The Undrowned

i.

here we see the insides
of a filmy, ghostly membrane.

what lingers under gauzy skin:
the perforated glow.

here we see a collection of ornaments:
fragile, tinseled, glass angels.

here we see the tacks and buttons
cast haphazardly.

here we see a pond where ripples
hint at things (un)drowned.

> *what is drowning*
> *when membranes*
>
> *like water are pierced*
> *and what gasps*
>
> *through the glistening*
> *puncture wound is air?*

zoom in and witness   *(quietly)*
a ritual disrobing:

the ghost of a woman pulls dew
from her hair. squishy, sun-licked pearls.

wipes her chin from what she has guzzled:
blood from the tap of a tree.

what was maple gave way      *(like lactation)*
to something more substantial.

this must be what they mean when they say, *she was not given what was wanted, but what was needed instead.*

ii.

I am a fish some days.
on others, the magpie
who starts and snatches air.

the air that spheres out
                                *one two three*
whenever I open my lips.

they call it oxygen.
they call these signs of life.
I call them rehearsals.

one of these days
I'll find the words.
then she can snatch at that.

bird-self, perch there
all you like.
you cannot hurry this.

iii.

besides, I am just here
in the shallows, drinking up the reeds.

a lily pad is bobbing
in my outstretched fingertips.

a cattail, bushy plume and hard stem,
catches on my right thumb.

and there is something rather
*regal* in this—don't you think?

orb and scepter
brought to me

by muck and chirping toads.
by red-winged blackbirds,

box turtles,
the gray and downy goslings.

and who would stop me
from self-coronating

sovereign of this pond?
who would still the trumpets

of the mauve mist
on its shore?

iv.

the queen of ponds
and dusk and mire rises
from the lakebed.

presses footprints into sand and
wrings out her dark gown.
fireflies crackle against star splatters

and this is her unending crown—
nothing as fixed or as dull as a bauble.
airy. windy. night.

she inhales and her contents dissolve,
leaving only the filament, the outline
of a queen. she exhales, re-solidifies.

a waxing, a waning, a tide.    *(and)*
what other power is there than this?
the landscape must rule itself.

watch love distill now, the sugar-crust drip.
nourishment oozing
from what was a wound.

v.

magpie, come and see
what I have pressed here in my palm.

for you, I have caught the dipping sun—
for you, I have made it a ruby.

wear it around your neck as a medal.
think of me and sing.

# Seeking Survival: Rapunzel

> *Someday, I'll have long, pretty hair.*
>
> —diary entry, age 17

I know, for I have seen it—I wrap it around my wrists
as I move through this forest. Strands of hair silver,
fine as spiderwebs. A human head the glinting ball
of yarn in this maze. A guiding rope, a ticker tape
I use to read your thoughts. I wind around trees
and crunch yellowed leaves underfoot
as birds titter above us. Your hair
is bright streamers, is carnival ribbons
adorning each branch. A garlanded aisle. Ceremony
almost bridal. I follow it, looping each yard
into spirals the size of a wasps' nest, a thick
boxer's cloth. At last, I arrive at your gravesite, your hair
gushing out from the small, pebbled mound.
Slowly, I kneel. I unglove myself. I cup earth and shovel
it sideways. I am digging for you. I am digging,
sweet child. I find your face and I exhume you.
You wrap your arms around my sorry neck;
you smile.

# The Angel of Dissociation
# Comes to Collect Me: Age 17

The angel steps through
shin-high grasses

wet with midnight dew.
The girl is stretched

on a trampoline
against indigo clouds.

Her eyes are closed.
Her lips are closed

and curved into a smile.
Her open palms

frame her head, make her
a human trident.

The angel sits down
with a squeaking of springs.

The dark canvas bends
to support her.

*I dreamt I was
disembodied*, the girl says.

*I dreamt I could feel
all things.*

## Cipher

The cat, for once, stays on her leash
and sits beside me in the driveway, purring.

I am turning another year older today.
I am stretching out my bare legs. I marinate

in sun. On my left, the spring grass has
already grown enormous. It wavers

like a twirled skirt in wind. On my right,
the dandelion tufts puff out like smoke breath,

exhaled from rounded lips. I have come here
to contemplate, a miniature pilgrimage, so small

it could tuck inside a hollow sugar egg. I have
crossed the tiny threshold from kitchen wood

to hot concrete in hopes of locating
transcendence. The cat yawns and gleams,

the light warms my shins, and a spider
half the size of my hand clutches the side

of the shed. We distance. We distance. My heart
is thrumming. I picture his leap and his bite.

But I stay here, back against the sliding glass door.
I stay here, watching petals fall like stirred-up

floral snow. I respect his presence. Respect
the threat. A creature known in Old English

as both *poison* and *weaver*. One who destroys and
connects. Ambiguous eight-legged cipher.

In plum-blossom air, I am afraid, but also,
as the pavement glows, peaceful. Reverent.

The spider is part of the scene, but so
is the cat, so is the garden. So am I.

## Parable

One summer, two kookaburras mated
on a power line, extinguishing light

in a thousand homes. Stories say
the female opened her wings

and touched two wires. Closing the circuit.
Making, of her body, a conductor. And his,

attached to hers. Witnesses gaped
at brilliant flashes, cacophony like drums.

The birds, when they hit the ground,
were dead. Coursing with currents of gold.

And O, prophetic valentine. God, make in me
the wire, the wingspan, the jubilant flare.

# The Angel of Dissociation Comes to Collect Me: Age [?]

The current carries them
far away, curves

and undulations of the road's
gray spine, its yellow vertebrae.

Trees disappear. Jackrabbits skitter
into holes under sun-scorched vines.

*Where are we going?* one girl asks.
She watches the mile markers

blur by. The angel has her aviator
sunglasses on. Her elbow catches

light out the window. *Not
to the afterlife*, the angel says, turning

the radio on. A soaring note
sounds. *Not to the afterlife just yet.*

The many girls lean on each
other for comfort. Music sails on.

In the rearview mirror, they see
the angel looks like them.

An angel of catching what falls
through cracks: a mythmaker, a soul.

## Seeing the Door

I turned around the corner
and saw the blue door, the one with the fresh
coat of paint we put on, and fragmented
into three. One was the current self, the one
standing under the honey locust tree with our
house key in hand. One was younger, 21, the girl
whose hair you brushed behind her ear, then added
a single forget-me-not there, a blue that stained
my heart. One was 18, the girl staring at a blue door
in a city far away, thinking, *Someday, I'd like to have
a door that blue—as vibrant, as cobalt as this.* All of this
happened in less than a second. Then the three of us
reintegrated into one, like a Slinky whose stretched ends
someone released. This reminds me we are
echo chambers, hallways of mirrors. Labyrinths
under our skin. I put the key in, rotate the handle,
and step into what I call home.

# Triptych

Sunday. The rain drips down
as if from some great beast. Shaking out
her coat. Her hair numen, the sky.

Inside, the furnace growls. Flexes
its flanks. The curled cat flicks her ear
in dreams, a little loaf. She lets

me stroke her hollow throat. I let
her claw my skin. I let you stroke
my hollow throat. And this is what rises

to trust in this world. You and I and she
and all your flannel are ephemeral. Still,
I incant. Hold this light in my hands.

# The Circle is Closed

I return to the place where I made the prayer
that changed my life forever. A girl in a scarf
in a coffee shop, opening her petals to wind.

I crossed the bridge and saw the ocean
gleam, a fresh-cut pear slice. Saw raindrops
console the pavement, soft-focus the lens.

I gather up the ghosts of all my selves, Hot Topic
hair-dyed. Gather up the twenty-somethings
tripping on rocks, on lies. Flush-cheeked, desolate.

I gather up the ghost of the girl who threw the ring in the lake.
And there it should have stayed, my friend.
And there, now, so it shall.

I wrap a coat around the girl who shivered on the corner.
Give her agrimony, give her deadly nightshade too.
Pluck the thank you off her tongue for the bundle of nettles

she had been handed, thinking it was a bouquet.
A pearl none of us asked for.
A pearl I feed to the sun.

I fold the ghosts inside the wooden wardrobe of forgiveness.
Wash their caked mascara off. Tuck them in
clean sheets. How long have I sought

the breadth of hands to gently press these doors shut?
I smooth the crease: an archivist, a caretaker, a spell.
A medium who hears, then blesses, what flickers, then departs.

Never again will I confuse the compass needle with the North.

## Second Wedding

It is a periwinkle day. The ivied
arch aglow with briar roses.
The bride's bouquet a cream
parfait, the groomsmen crisp
as notes. It is a second
wedding, and you and I watch:
I, freshly unmarried. A gesture
of faith in unknown
shores. A paper boat placed
on the sea. I take your hand
as we see them rise to the
vastness of it, the wind's teeth.
We rise to the enormity of it,
the boundless sky called love.

# Brunch Dress

The brunch dress is starburst gold,
flecked with milk-white blossoms.
Short sleeves. A swooping V-neck
held with a single clasp. Always,
in the brunch dress, I'm a little
afraid of showing too much
rib cage—like the top of my
heart will peer over the rim and
be spotted: a rogue red bird.

Here I am eating French toast
dappled in caramel sauce,
ripe sliced banana. Here I am
sharing coffee with you,
blowing on the hot, dark pool.
No one must know how
hard I am trying to not feel like
a novice. How natural
I want to appear in this languid
café scene. Be honest
with me: does this hope
make my eyes look
ravenous? Suit my lip
shade? Can a hermit crab woman
grow into a new shell? Fill
its shape with light?

I'll be honest with you: I believe
in horizons that stretch as if
waking from cat naps. Believe
in cutting an audacious mold
and pouring myself in.

# Happy Cat

There's a yip down the hall, a shriek
of elation. You say, *What a happy cat.*
I say, *I think it was a baby.* We laugh at this.
We hear her toddle by. Nevertheless,
each time we hear her yelp, we say, *Oh! Happy*
*cat.* It becomes automatic, a reflex we share,
a set of words that rearrange the world.
We are building a lexicon, building
a life. Barn-raising with small deeds.

I made a home once and it scattered like a barrel
hit with cannonballs. Made a home once
and it dripped like a waxwork cooked underneath
a hairdryer. This could stop me. It could stop me
right in my tracks. But I paw forward cautiously.
The happy cat is with me, a spirit we invented
who winds around my shins, whose purr assures
me: *Press your face into the blanket you use; let this*
*be the net that receives you. The net you weave*
*when falling is the brightest one of all.* I press my face
into the woolen braids, the queen-size breadth
its own landscape. In dreams, I patchwork
happy creatures, stitched from salvaged scraps.

# Fulgurite

Shocking, sparking, a bolt pours
from the sky and strikes
the earth. Electrifying

soot and sand, fusing them
to glass. The trace it leaves
is hollow, tubular—branched

as reaching hands. A network
of tunnels, spaces that were
not there before. Labyrinthine.

This is what you create in me,
world. Through jolts of searing
awe. You plunge this lightning

into me, place mazes in its wake.
And so I am a collection of
crystal, a sphere shot through

with fording. Like this, I become
a heart that singes and sings,
full of luminous paths.

# Notes

The "three eels" joke mentioned in "My Soul Shudders In and Out of My Body Like a Microscope In and Out of Focus" originated with a viral Tweet by @JNalv.

"Shotgunning" refers to one person breathing smoke into the mouth of another.

In "Torch," the game of blackjack is mentioned. A player says "Hit me" to indicate that they want another card added to their hand. Because of the game's rules, this can be a risky move. Also, as an update to this poem, Captain Cal is doing well. He lives with two adopted sisters, Goldie and Poppy, named for a type of flower said to bloom after a wildfire.

The agrimony in "The Circle is Closed" is inspired by a line from Lisa Loeb's "Furious Rose."

# Acknowledgments

Gratitude is extended to the editors of the following publications in which these poems first appeared, some in earlier forms and under earlier titles:

*Bad Pony*: Third section of "What I Mean"

*Breadcrumbs Magazine*: "The Angel of Dissociation Comes to Collect Me: Age 12"

*Burnt Offering* (Porkbelly Press, 2020): "Seeking Survival: Snow White"

*CLASH*: "Baby Ghost"

*COG*: "Purgatory," "Domesticity," "Mosaicists," and "Triptych"

*Colorado Review*: "Eden" and "Parable"

*Corvid Queen*: "Seeking Survival: Vasilisa the Beautiful"

*Crab Fat Magazine*: "The Undrowned"

*Fairy Tale Review*: "Seeking Survival: Cinderella"

*Femspec* (13.1): "Pomegranate Seeds"

*Fourteen Hills*: "Glitter Camo Girl" and "Beacon"

*Gingerbread House Lit Mag*: "Seeking Survival: Little Red Riding Hood"

*Haunted* (Lit Sisters, 2019): "The Angel of Dissociation Comes to Collect Me: Age 21"

*Idaho Press Tribune*: "Cipher"

*Iron Horse Literary Review*: "Small City Garden"

*Luna Luna Magazine*: "Family Ghost" and "River Ghost"

*Marathon Literary Review*: "Shotgunning"

*Mississippi Review*: "Fairy Tale with an AR-15"

*Moonsick Magazine*: Second section of "What I Mean"

*Pensive: A Global Journal of Spirituality and the Arts*: "Home/world" and "My Soul Shudders In and Out of My Body Like a Microscope In and Out of Focus"

*Rag Queen Periodical*: First section of "What I Mean"

*The Pinch*: "How to Tell the Angel of Cohesion That the Boy She Keeps Asking About Did Something Bad to You"

*Quail Bell Magazine*: "Singing Ghost"

*#WATERTOME* (White Stag Press, 2020): "Subaquatic"

*Winter Tangerine*: "Seeking Survival: The Little Mermaid"

*Witch Craft Magazine*: "The Angel of Dissociation Comes to Collect Me: Age 23"

*Writers in the Attic: Fuel* (The Cabin, 2019): "Prom Witch"

An earlier version of "Seeking Survival: The Snow Queen" first appeared in the chapbook *Coronations* (Ghost City Press, 2019). The Cinderella, Little Mermaid, and Vasilisa "Seeking Survival" poems appeared there as well, in earlier forms. "The Circle is Closed," "Second Wedding," "Brunch Dress," and "Happy Cat" first appeared in the chapbook *Simple Magic* (Ghost City Press, 2022).

———————

Thank you to each and every person who had a hand in the creation of this book. Though the majority of these poems were written between 2017 and 2020, the oldest one is from 2012, and the newest one is from 2022, so truly, thank you to everyone who helped shepherd them along during their journey. If you have ever encouraged me or my writing, please know that I am grateful.

Specifically, thank you to Chen Chen, Jennifer Militello, Allison Titus, Paige Ackerson-Kiely, and Sarah Manguso for their excellent mentorship and guidance. Thank you to Anaïs Duplan for selecting "Triptych" as the winner of the 2019-2020 COG Poetry Award, Adam Clay for selecting "Fairy Tale with an AR-15" as a finalist for the 2021 Mississippi Review Prize, and the editors of *The Pinch* for selecting "How to Tell the Angel of Cohesion That the Boy She Keeps Asking About Did Something Bad to You" (under an earlier title) as a finalist for the Spring 2021 Pinch Literary Awards. Thank you to the Alexa Rose Foundation, The Two Eight, Surel's Place, and the Covid Cultural Commission Fund— including Treefort Music Fest, the Velma V. Morrison Center for Performing Arts, the City of Boise, and the Boise City Department of Arts & History—for the gift of time to work on these poems. Thank you to DigiPen Institute of Technology for nourishing me as a writer. Thank you to the entire editorial team at Cornerstone Press for showing such immense care for this book.

Thank you to my family for their love and support, especially my mom Diane, who read and generously held space for many different versions of the manuscript. Thank you to Alex for reading it, asking questions, and saying you wanted to know more—thank you for always understanding my heart, and for holding it so gently. Thank you to Shilo for the encouragement, companionship, and walks in the winter—your bravery and tenderness inspire me. Hannah, thank you for the many coffee meetups where we workshopped poems and talked about dreams—these are memories I will cherish forever. Thank you to Jason for constantly reminding me of the power, depth, and beauty of literature—reading and writing with you brings me joy.

Thank you to Kerri, Katie, Megan, Laura, CL, Emily, Reverie, Lee, Danielle, Nichole, Bonnie, Jake, Cole, Kevin, Lynne, Jana, Alissa, Carl, Ryan, Darren, Michael, and others who kindly gave feedback on several of these pieces in their early stages. To the many friends who helped see me through a difficult chapter to a happier one—Lessie, Jenn, Jenny, Wendy, Cristina, Lisa, Stefanie, Mical, Tess, Kyle, and Lila, just to name a few—thank you for your strength, and thank you for leading by example. Knowing you believed in me helped me believe in myself.

Finally, to the cat who appears in several of these poems, thank you for your feisty and too-brief life. I wish we had gotten more time. Your memory glows like a lantern in my heart.

CATHERINE KYLE is the author of *Shelter in Place* (2019) and other poetry collections. Her writing has appeared in *Bellingham Review*, *Colorado Review*, *Mid-American Review*, and other journals. She was the winner of the 2019-2020 COG Poetry Award, a finalist for the 2021 Mississippi Review Prize in poetry, and a finalist for the 2021 Pinch Literary Awards. She is an assistant professor at DigiPen Institute of Technology, where she teaches creative writing and literature.

www.ingramcontent.com/pod-product-compliance
Lightning Source LLC
Chambersburg PA
CBHW020425130626
46549CB00006B/2744